VOICES FOR CHANGE

Copyright © 2020 for each verse belongs to the author of that verse

The right of the authors to be identified as the authors of the verses within this book has been asserted by them in accordance with the Copyright, Designs and Patents Act 1998.

All rights reserved.

All rights reserved. No part of this publication may be reproduced, stored in or introduced into a retrieval system or transmitted, in any form, or by any means (electronic, mechanical, photocopying, recording or otherwise) without the prior written permission of the publisher or unless such copying is done under a current Copyright Licensing Agency license. Any person who does any unauthorised act in relation to this publication may be liable to criminal prosecution and civil claims for damages.

VOICES FOR CHANGE

Edited by

ANNE BARR, SUZANNAH EVANS
and DANUTA KOT

First Published in 2020 by Fantastic Books Publishing

Cover design by Gabi

ISBN (ebook): 978-1-912053-39-1
ISBN (paperback): 978-1-912053-38-4

Dedication

This collection is dedicated to the memories of Mary Sarjeant and Ken Reah

Mary Sarjeant, known to many of her friends as Mary Marshall (1950-2018)

An alumnus of Sheffield Girls' High School, Mary was a Sheffielder through and through. She was a campaigner all her life, for women's rights and animal welfare, access to arts education and support for those with mental health difficulties, and latterly, for the protection of Sheffield's healthy street trees. Her support for #SaveSheffTrees was steadfast, and despite long term illness, she'd jump in a taxi at the drop of a hat, and travel all over the city, in order to sit under threatened trees to prevent them being felled. Mary was always a champion of political, social and environmental justice, and her frustration with Sheffield City Council's contract to fell healthy street trees in her beloved green city, inspired her to join the It's Our City! campaign at its inception. In the last few weeks of her life, Mary insisted on helping devise the original *It's Our City!* pledges for the May 2018 local elections, and would have been thrilled that the petition reached its required number of signatures. Shortly before Mary died in July 2018, she talked of how she wasn't afraid of death. She was proud of her life and what she'd achieved, and felt she'd done all she needed to do here. She firmly believed she was now needed somewhere else. Thank you, Mary, for your passion, commitment and friendship. You were and always will be a true 'Sheffield Woman of Steel'.

Ken Reah (1929 – 2019)

Ken came to Sheffield in his late forties to work at the university, and became an enthusiastic Sheffielder. He loved the contrasts the city offered, and he loved its parks and green spaces. An artist and writer, he dedicated an exhibition held in Sheffield University library to paintings of Endcliffe Park, where he walked every day. He kept up his habit of walking there up to a fortnight before his death. His poems in this anthology include Two Poems for Summer, which reflect his love of the park, and of Sheffield.

Voices for Change

This anthology of poetry, Voices for Change, arose from a campaign in the City of Sheffield for more democracy in the way the city was run.

Sheffield City Council operates what is known as the 'strong leader' model. Under this system, a small number of councillors, ten out of eighty-four in this case, have the power and responsibility to make nearly all the major decisions on behalf of over half a million people. Despite, or maybe because of this model, the council made a series of decisions that seemed to go against what the people of the city wanted, and yet there was no mechanism for changing these.

In 2018, a group of Sheffielders decided to campaign for a referendum to allow the people of Sheffield to vote and decide under what system they wanted the council to run: the strong leader model, or a more democratic committee system that would give local people more voice and make greater use of the skills and experience of all the councillors. In the course of the year, the campaign collected over 26,000 signatures which meant that the council had to call a referendum and ask the people how they wanted the city to be run.

This anthology, Voices for Change, arose from this campaign. We asked the people of Sheffield to write poems that expressed their views about the city they live in. The poems could relate to individual experience, or be about the city and the people themselves.

This anthology contains a selection of those poems – the voices of the people of Sheffield, expressing their love for the city that is their home.

Contents

Introduction by Ian McMillan	xi
Benjamin Zephaniah	1
Lovely Trees	1
Rachel Bower	3
Women of Steel	3
Seven Hills	5
Alan Payne	7
Surrey Street	7
Rony Robinson	9
The Carpenter and the Thief	9
Rob Macfarlane	13
Heartwood	13
Kate Rutter	15
Hard Shoulder	15
Benoit	17
Voice-ity	17
Betty Allsorts	19
The Wonderful Everyday	19
Carl Douglas	21
Pride of the North	21
Claire Brockman	23
Sheffield University November 1976	23
Cora Greenhill	25
Seen in Sheffield	25
Poetry in The Bath	26
David Stead	27
MAYDAY! MAYDAY!	27
Hillsborough Echoes (After Carol Ann Duffy)	29
Derek Agar	31
The Voices of Hallam	31
Andrew Senior	33
Maureen and the Machines	33
We Are Sheffield	34

Jane Monach	37
On the Bole Hills	37
Jenny Hockey	39
Going to Bed with the Moon	39
January Hallelujah	40
Stitch in Time	41
Jill Angood	43
Let's Hear It for Street Trees	43
Nether Edge Haiku	44
Katharine Towers	45
The Scream	45
Linda Goulden	47
A View From Carsick Hill	47
Martin Parsons	49
Sheffield: Split City	49
Nicky Hallett	51
Sound Tracks	51
Veronica Fibisan	53
Dandelion Distribution	53
Ken Reah	55
Two poems for Summer	55
A Dying	56
Bronwen Barber	57
A Clean Life	57
Abbeydale Industrial Hamlet, 31 August	58
The Price of an Abbeydale Scythe	59
Jane Sharp	61
Life on the X17	61
Off His Head	64
Paul Carnell	65
At Brincliffe Edge	65
Beggar	65
But if (In response to What If by Andrew Motion on the side of the Hallam Building)	66
Charlotte Ansell	67

Queen of the North	67
In hope	68
Made in Sheffield	69
Rita Willow	71
Anti – Advert (to HSBC's Poem Ad)	71
Built for Purpose	72
On My Doorstep	73
Molly Meleady-Hanley	75
It's Our City Too – Our Voice and Rights Matter Too	75
Joyce M Bullivant	77
Liberty stands among us all	77
Sally Goldsmith	79
Fairytale	79
Retreat to Forest Hill, 2018	80
The Alder, Sheffield 2017	81
Shirley Cameron	83
Endcliffe Park	83
Sharrow Festival in Sheffield	84
The Sheaf from the Train	84
It's Our City writers' workshop	85
It's Our City!	85
About It's Our City!	87

Introduction by Ian McMillan

Here are the New Maps

In his poem in this anthology 'The Carpenter and the Thief' Rony Robinson asks 'who makes the history' and in these pages you'll find that question asked many many times as poets grapple with life in a city that finds itself again and again on the cusp of change and reinvention.

Poets dream of conversations here, and they imagine blacksmiths waking the past; they meet people washed up against subway walls and they have visions of the city bare-shouldered and hard. In each of these poems each of these poets draws their own new and personal map of a city and each of these maps re-emphasises that the local can always become the universal and that a city we thought we knew well can be illuminated anew when poets shine their lights on it.

The book examines a city that has been examined many times by politicians and planners and visionaries and urbanists and academics and educationalists and historians and sociologists but the book gazes at the place in a different way because it lets the poets loose in it. They make their own maps, they take us to new places and they show us the parts of the old places we've never seen before.

All a poet has is the alphabet; here is an A to Z of Sheffield, presented by those who know.

Benjamin Zephaniah

Lovely Trees

Lovely trees are being cut to death
by remote suited folk.
My heart's with those
that walk the streets
and the old great Vernon Oak.

Rachel Bower

Women of Steel

We are sisters who clank through the streets
on rustless feet and chain linked arms
the deep pull of ore in our loins –
calls of ancestors deep in the rocks of yolk and plum and rust
I polish her toes till they shine –
she deserves this at least and I know that she'd polish mine.

We are women of steel
women who do what we feel
women who do what we can
women who cry, women who rise
women at the heart of this town.

My nipples leak steel milk
and she keeps holding me up.

We are women who labour and birth
women who work, women who juggle
dark peaks and light, women who do what we can
when Cleethorpes' too dear there's the beach in town
the patch of sand that scratches our palms
sisters of steel squatting down.

I wipe orange streams from her cheeks
and keep holding her up.

We are women of steel
of hijabs and braids, of curly and straight
of blond hair and white
women who run, women who ride
women who lathe and grind
without gloves, we are women of three kids and twins on the way
and *just a bit of peace*

just a bit of peace please

She wipes crystal dust from my nails
and keeps holding me up.

We are women of hills
of limestone and grit
of ups and downs
of you can do it duck
we'll get through it
we are women who nobody knows
guilt plated girls with lacquered legs
women of glad rags
of red crags, of sneaking bags back
from the foodbank
we are women of steel

I grip her shoulder
and keep holding her up.

women who do what we feel
women who do what we can
women who cry, women who rise
women at the heart of this town.

Seven Hills
Sheffield, Ibadan, Rome

They say this city is built on seven hills. If you get high
enough you might see them, sleeping dinosaurs, streets
sloping up and down jewelled tails, wings, thighs:
tramped them every day to school and work, but our feet

know only boils, lumps, spots; small cuts and grazes
as we push prams up, plastic bags cutting blades into fingers
on the way down; as we pop to the shop for milk, papers,
a chat with the grocer, as we drive to the cemetery, linger

with violets for the lost. We know of seven sisters, sins,
wonders, but what we live here is the surprise white
of magnolia in late winter, diamond sparkle on the bins,
melting jigsaws of ice, raw hands and chins from biting

winds, the annual battle of magpie and crow
disputing the nest again, oblivious of those hills below.

Alan Payne

Surrey Street

On the pavement near the door
to the Central Library,
someone has chalked:

> *Watch*
> *your*
> *step*

I can just see myself tripping
and falling into a hidden well.

I can just see myself tripping
and falling into a secret cave.

I can just see myself tripping
and falling into another world.

I can just see myself tripping
and tumbling into an abyss.

Further along the pavement,
outside the Winter Gardens,
more words, same handwriting:

> *Man/Lady*
> *What*
> *now?*

Rony Robinson

The Carpenter and the Thief
for Charlie Peace and Edward Carpenter

Listen
learn from history
two dead men in old Fargate
in 1878
getting up to fight

>One in sandals
>one's a scandal
>one asks why
>one why not
>one's a poet
>one is not

But what can we learn from history
now everybody's dead

>One's tall
>one's Trinity Hall
>one's Darn-all
>one was a vicar
>one was a nicker
>one wrote books denouncing the boss
>one goosed a wife up a jennel at old Banner
>Cross

>You say your poem's set
>In 1878
>then these dead men
>could never have met
>in old Fargate

I say ask who makes the history
is it the teacher in the schools

where they teach you how to stutter
and teach you poems must rhyme
all the time
and that history is for the old
and you must never ask
whose histories don't get told

> One played classical piano in his kitchen for
> vegetarian swingers
> one played skipping fiddle with his only three
> fingers
> one died in Leeds jail
> no surprise
> after saying he'd finish his breakfast bacon if
> the hangman didn't mind damn his eyes
> one died in Surrey
> no surprise
> forgetting the words of his *England Arise*

There's no according to history
let's change history
don't read history
write it

> One believed in redistributing
> one redistributed
> one couldn't marry, it would have been a crime
> one usually had two wives at a time

History does not record
that Ted and Charlie ever met
history does not record
most of our lives
and yet –

> See here together
> the gurning burglar
> and the naked vicar –
> the Thief and the Carpenter

History does not write itself
to be left for ever on some dusty shelf
someone's paid the piper

        So be weird
        sport a beard
        be in and out
        and wave it all about
        wear Jesus' boots
        booze
        steel yourself
        steal, yourself
        dream, yourself

        dare not to fit in sometimes

and your poems don't have to rhyme or reason if you don't want them to and they can go all over the page and you don't even need to understand them yourself or have capital letters or punctuations or lines that line up because you can be like walt whitman (or edward carpenter of course) and just keep writing till you want to stop because you don't have to make sense if you don't want to any more

        Get in there
        strip to your underwear
        proudly share
        Your family jewels
        and your Sheffield thywels
        hear the voice of changes everywhere
        (for a change)

who decides history has to be true
who decides what happens next

        and who decides how long a poem must be
        before it can stop
        and start again

Listen
learn from history
two dead men in old Fargate
in 1878
getting up to fight

Rob Macfarlane

Heartwood

Would you hew me
To the heartwood, cutter?
Would you leave me open-hearted?
Put an ear to my bark, cutter,
Hear my sap's mutter,
Mark my heartwood's beat,
My leaves' flutter.
Would you turn me to timber, cutter?
Leave me nothing but a heap of logs,
A pile of brash?
I am a world, cutter,
I am a maker of life –
Drinker of rain, breaker of rocks,
Caster of shade, eater of sun,
I am time-keeper,
Breath-giver,
Deep-thinker, cutter;
I am a city of butterflies,
A country of creatures.
But my world takes years to grow,
Cutter, and seconds to crash;
Your saw can fell me,
Your axe can bring me low.
Do you hear these words I utter?
I ask this of you
Have you heartwood, cutter?
Have those
Who sent you?

Kate Rutter

Hard Shoulder

Driving down the Parkway, our headlights
frisking trees right and left, what lies
beyond the green verge is anybody's guess.

Half-asleep I dream industrial estates,
hyper-markets, places that call themselves mills
and are not mills. One day we will turn off.

We duck under the flyover, choose one of three
equidistant routes past staggering girls
in the night club dawn and the blue-lit waterfall

marooned in nowhere that lights up squatting
homeless boys we are too afraid to house.

Benoit

Voice-ity

"Do remember while the gone days,
that we mattered 'bout our old ways.
n that through prosper or scarcity,
we've all now made what's this city.

•••

As much as new, with time decays,
as such we grew, here or away.
(I)t ain't like we aren't electricity,
we're part of the current of this city.

•••

That's important, what each would say.
What can or can't, together we may
discuss our issues, in security,
share visions of me and yous, in our city."

Betty Allsorts

The Wonderful Everyday

On a body's length of cardboard undone
and laid out on the pavement he sleeps
head to the billboard and toe to nothing.
All night the poster couple sipped coffee at his head.
They drink on into morning in their box of light
where all a life might need is slowly spun
by power that could better make him a brew.
Home is the Most Important Place in the World.
Behind the billboard his neighbour sleeps
head-to-head like in the beds each side of walls
in Sheffield's tight terraces.
He has no walls. For a few shuddering frames
the window of the bus makes an inside-out room
and then we're gone. The billboard life reels on.
The Wonderful Everyday is Coming.

Carl Douglas

Pride of the North

The sky stretches out: red, yellow and grey, that's how it was, back in the day, the drop hammer furnaces thundered away, 24/7 through the night and the day. White lightning metal this city has forged, a byword for quality at home and abroad.

Sheffield held firm and weathered the storm, showing its mettle through both World Wars, the Women of Steel and those men of valour, all pulled together in those darkest hours. Such steely resolve was witnessed again, when they each stood their ground and our proud trees were saved.

No longer silenced or too quickly ignored, with those cranes and that miner, we look up to them all.

They peak from the Pennines and look down from the Moors, Sheffield has risen to shoulder them all, five rivers run through it and converge on the Don, to power the wheels where the hard work went on.

In small draughty workshops young mesters were taught, their goods now displayed in our own Cutlers Hall. The birthplace of football, and centre for sport, the first home of snooker and Olympic Ponds Forge.

That 'Shed on the corner?' a working police Tardis, the Commonside voices bring echoes of Jarvis. Cut from a diamond, compact and neat, surrounded by gardens and so close to the Peaks.

The Peoples' own theatre, their words on the page, thrust into the spotlight on the Crucible stage. Marvellous museums, libraries and parks, nightclubs and restaurants with numerous bars.

The Central Cathedral, mosques and broad churches, the new city market and those places of learning, a city of sanctuary for people displaced, not judged by their colour, gender or faith.

Actors, musicians, writers and artists, they all know that Sheffield is where their real heart is. The Dales are inviting, I'll give you that – but you should take in the views from those Park Hill Flats.

With our pavement of stars and the Meadow Hall Dome, people are proud to call Sheffield their home. Sir Michael Palin and those Arctic Monkeys, we showcase most films and those documentaries.

It may seem like a puzzle but the pieces all fit, once you've splashed some of Hendo's on your fresh fish and chips, it's a city of culture – but we don't go with the flow; we march to our own beat and let the world know.

Still rough round the edges, let's not pretend, but if you come as a stranger you will return as a friend, two teams now united with one common goal, no walls only bridges – in a place to call home.

Five rivers converge becoming the Don, we retain northern values which we choose to pass on, the White Rose of Yorkshire will always be flown, in this city of Sheffield, a place to call home.

That drop forge hammer falls silent today, trams travel to Rotherham not just Halfway, we fight our own corner – that's the way we've been taught, in this city of Sheffield, pride of the North.

Claire Brockman

Sheffield University November 1976

Students in duffel coats with pointed hoods
Like animated charcoal crayons
Sharpened, grey and pencil-slim
Go hurrying through the rain, book-laden
Soaked by spray, and splashed by glistening puddles.
City shoes slide upon the water polished pavement, and the leaves,
Whilst umbrellas blossom here and there
Like tropical flowers, swaying in a grey monsoon.

Cora Greenhill

Seen in Sheffield

This is what boys are for! To strip
to the hip-sagging baggy pants;
shrug, slouch, then somersault to the brim
of the fountain; cat crawl the wall,
cartwheel, lazy-vault a stone plinth,
bend knees and flat foot it free-style,
down the stepped seven levels
of stone slabs sliced by blades of water.

This is what boys do: brace
on the handrail of city steps, spring
so that two feet lunge up to stand
on the next rail. Let go, drop back, land
squarely in size 12s on the pavement.
Stroll back to the crowd, unflinching,
unsmiling, like no one's watching. Cool
as this cutting edge curve of water on steel.

This is what public sculpture's for: to mirror
these moves. This is what public spaces are for.
This is what this Saturday afternoon's for:
sliding down stone bannisters on one hip,
September not quite here. This
is what boys are: poems freed in air
above the sandwich wrappers in Sheaf Square,
break-falling among pigeons.

Poetry in The Bath

Snuggled in the heart of the pub,
held in the crook of the street's arm,
we bed down, hot as the fat
sausage rolls they serve in the bar.

The door yawns gently inwards.
The board we made to fit the hatch
is beginning to lose its seal. Poems
rise and ring over a hubbub of pub talk.

One summer night, Morris dancers
played their clackety clack
on the pavement outside.
We almost gave up. Not quite.

When time is called, we find
some lines have stayed, like friends,
to cheer us, soothe or sting us,
or sing on the lonely road home.

David Stead

MAYDAY! MAYDAY!

As I walked out one May morning
green Devonshire's mud waste
the urban-canyoned stores on
dog-legged Division Street

Pace on pace Sheffield's Seville tower
loomed larger into view
its great brass bell boomed High Noon hour …
Malachite, polar-hued

hawk-eyed, helmed, twice-bolted Vulcan
stark on malign nimbus
cranked grim gaze round razed Peace Gardens
pole-axed Fargate, dauntless

fire-stormed Star clock, Old Town Hall ridge
so-crowned still, Wain's motte gone
from long watch over Lady's Bridge
where guardless now flowed Don …

While petty pace crept on past
Balm's bare pole to the dead
of Armageddon, Gaumont masked
in red-brick burqa, Peck's

ghosts scratched vinyl pianos jangling—
Sudden stunning civic
gallows its three hanged men dangling
kicking grim and gothic

as George pinioned Patrick the pair
spread-eagled Andrew three
boxed hapless compass in thin air
a lesser Calvary

one-gibbet Trinity … They swayed
half-masted red white blue
that bleak 5th day of malvine May
In nineteen eighty-two

and far away midst grim green hills
of southern whale's way's waste
invincible destiny's mills
ground heedless without haste

ground small. Hull down on Falkland's rim
a sinking steel ship named
with our Steel City's eponym
burned hissed flared seethed – proclaimed

To dust and Eros *O, you who*
Wreak wrong on others learn!
Wretchedness will be wrought on you
by others in return!

Hillsborough Echoes (After Carol Ann Duffy)

Two small crowds in one pub that Saturday
in April eighty-nine. One shares its name.
The other mirrors their hope – to win the game.
They kick off in two hours! – two miles away.

But now the passing honours, now displays
of pride. First Merseyside's young hearts, that burn.
The *Forests* grin and bear it, wait their turn …
The *Nottingham*, that semi-final day.

And every one would have a memory
of how they met last year. *Will this year be
the Double? Or Quits?* They all walked on, to see!

•••

Stone-boxed, back home. Perched high on terraced edge
my attic view: the Don; green park; that stadium
whose sound waves lap this *Crescent* auditorium –
from that shoebox, crouched blue on my window ledge?

Sense kick-off. *Hear those chants! Wait for that glorious
Ground swell that hails attack; roars ecstatic* –
Cut off. To dead ball – not yet ominous …
Along the Mersey now it's very late.
Phone-boxed mothers; children; partners; wives; mates – still cry.
For each of them, the clock will too long be
stopped dead at fifteen minutes after three.
But none of us can ever say *Goodbye!* –
Without the truth and justice we all wait.

Derek Agar

The Voices of Hallam

Vulcan stands proudly above the town hall clock
A symbol of Sheffield's strength and pride
While, unseen below, callous plans are unlocked
Which breed much confusion, and citizens divide

Sheffield's attractions are many and green
Europe's biggest village, they say,
With leafy suburbs which trees help to clean
And parks which are verdant and places to play

Sheffield has waterways between seven hills
Loxley, Porter, Rivelin and Sheaf
Arterial clearways of long history and mills
They flow into the Don, their chief

Sheffield's heritage is under great threat
From those with no soul or sense of connect
The reason for outrage the leaders don't get
They're happy to see what's valuable wrecked

Sheffield the emerging city of the sixties
Has become lately the site of a battle
Citizens who care have taken steps risky
To react to council bluster and prattle

It's not just the trees, it's the parks and the history
The old town hall and the castle the same
Birley Spa, its sale is to locals a mystery,
The old things of value, to sell them's the aim

The Vernon Oak and the Chelsea Elm
Silent predecessors of urban sprawl
Innocent targets of council stupidity
False accountancy, clear to all

But the conscience of Hallam can now be heard
Enough is enough, say the gathering voices
Heroic defenders have recently stirred
And made clear more viable choices

It's more than trees now, it's how things are run
It's how do we tell what's false and what's true,
The key facts are hidden from the light of the sun
Denied to the many and locked away by the few.

Thanks to the grass roots, heroic and few,
The thoughts of the many have stirred
We're now more informed of what's really true
And how our leaders have erred

Thanks to those who started the fight
And pointed out what was worth saving
And how our leaders must guard Sheffield's rights
And at last stop their crass misbehaving

Andrew Senior

Maureen and the Machines

Maureen hated the machine
that beeped and the automated ever-pleasant
lady and the red flashing light when an alcohol purchase
was taking place and the spatter of loose change and the backs of heads
and no receipts because the machines were taking over as far as she could see
and behind her counter she felt quite forgotten and sometimes lonely and spent
a considerable portion of her shift pushing dust
along the edges of her till.

We Are Sheffield

Did you hear me when
The roads were being dug up
When the pneumatic drills sang
When the wrecking balls swung into concrete
To rearrange our city centre
Like it was just a show home?
Did you hear me when
I conquered the seven hills
When I was wild with victory
When I found love in the valleys
Overcome by the green goodness of it all?
Will you hear me when
A single tree falls
When I stumble on the road and into a pothole
When my streetlight goes out
When the bus doesn't show
And I am left at the mercy of the Shiregreen wind
And the Birley rain?
Do you wonder why
I keep asking the question?
You need to know that for every one of me
There's another on the next street
On the next seat
Thinking what I'm thinking
Speaking what I'm speaking
The voice you're hearing
Is not mine
It's ours
And we are saying something unambiguous
To the smooth surfaces
To the strong leaders
To the cracked pavements, smashed shelters
Rubble and rusting girders
To those who say they speak for us

We are the wasted talent
The bottom up
Half a million thinkers, talkers, workers
The wall breakers
We are the goodwill
The heartbeat
We are the city
We are Sheffield

Jane Monach

On the Bole Hills
Friday 30 December 2016

Winter sun brings steel-grey shimmer to worn arms of a park bench,
memorial to a local lover of the place, which peers silently towards Rivelin,
towards thick woods in the valley's dip, towards folded hills and wide sky.

Along the path to Crookes, trees naked and branched against the sky,
wait till Spring to be dressed again.

Two runners breathe past me, their busy legs rhythmed
like mine were years ago. Dogs bound,
race the large expanse of grass that hosted Sunday football matches,
and now soaks up the sweat and discipline of rugby.

Playground murmurs float down the winding paths to lower Walkley,
out over Stannington. Small bodies weave through climbing frames,
sit in square swings, avoid prams and tricycles steered by adults.
A lone explorer climbs the grassy slope right up to the railings,
out of her mother's sight against the low bright glare.

The zip wire below shakes a rag-doll shape along its tautness with a whoosh.
The banked slide, safe and gleaming, spews out bundles on to soft ground,
not the hard tarmac my children's bones knew.

Further on, rocks of old quarry works, solid, jagged, shining now,
much-used as ships' bows, and jump-off points *to infinity and beyond*,
locations of crash landings, limbs cracked in icy snow of colder times,
when trays and sledges lost control, scattered bodies, shrieks and screams.

Today all sounds seem muted by the sun, the hillside
in a tranquil mood until the wind comes.

Jenny Hockey

Going to Bed with the Moon

Startled by a moon-scuffed sky,
I lean my head to the window—
caught on a shredding of cloud,
its wounded twist and drift—
stand like the badger
stitched on my Japanese silk,
snout raised to the stars,
belly floodlit
until the moon desists
from taunting our trees,
unleaved, sky high.
Moon – wan as an egg,
shadows my heels up the stairs,
climbs the folds of my sheets.

January Hallelujah

Praise to the Lord of lights not on,
of Weetabix spooned in the shadow
of a candle, Lord of the drizzle
that haunts the back of our house.
Praise to the Lord of macs,
of waterproof trousers, velcro
and zips, to the Lord of low expectations—
of just getting out
to bring the mud back in,
rain-spattered glasses, hair
in a frizz, praise him
for deafness to grumbles,
the whine of a child that builds to a roar,
who won't let bumface boss her
but does, who sings in the rain, hand
in a grownup hand, sparking her brother
to fragments of husky pop,
words we never quite catch.

Stitch in Time

When you come back to knitting
later in life, you know your needles
and your mother's needles before you
will have to be found, maybe behind
the hoover and the wellington boots
in the understairs cupboard
and when you find them – by chance –
all their sizes will be history, superseded
by both a metric and an American system
and the knitting patterns you find on sale
will suit only the fragile girls who haunt
a pebbled Hebridean beach or wilt
about grouse moors, pale and lost to love
while you stand squat by *The Wool-Baa*
– hours to go before opening time,

eyeing yarn for socks you promised yourself
not to knit, after too many nights on the sofa,
your loved ones withdrawn to their beds
and their books, while you can no longer
resist, impelled to a row that you know
will not be your last or your last or your last
now you've come back to knitting.

Jill Angood

Let's Hear It for Street Trees

Let's celebrate our street trees
    filters of exhausted air
    leaves dulled grey by dust
    roots choked by coke and beer cans
    bark-scarred but valiant
Let's celebrate our street trees
    as they raise the green flag for spring's getaway
    sport a blaze of blowzy reds and yellows
    to warn us of winter
    play host to the dark flying things of night
    and the hidden congress of fungi and algae
    which lies at the heart of life for all
    tempting us to climb up and upwards
    into the flickering leaf-light
Let's celebrate our street trees
    sturdy Canutes against the tides
    of tarmac and traffic
    their leaves gently rustling
Yes, let's celebrate our street trees!

Nether Edge Haiku

Brown- ridged bark stubbled
with grey orange lichen, white
brackets of fungi

Hosts to the flying
things of night and day, bees
bats and butterflies

Trees flicker gently
Jerky old movies with their
soundtracks of water

Sputnik flowered tree
strangler, ivy, poisonous
but bee-beloved

Above me the dance of
light and leaves, no stillness
except in my heart

Autumn flounces red
tatters, tossed by the wind, warn
of nakedness to come

Katharine Towers

The Scream

A man is not screaming.
He lives in the loud world
and, oh, he is afraid.

He has neither father nor mother.
The world took them away.
He has forgotten their voices and fingers.

He has neither sister nor brother.
The world took them away in a boat.
He has forgotten their lies by the water.

The world goes into his mouth.
It tastes of gravel and grass,
the brimstone tongues of the dead.

His mouth will not close.
His eyes will not look
into the mouth of the cave.

Pity his long drawn-out body.
Pity his soul in its ashes and smoke.
Pity a man in the deep well.

Linda Goulden

A View From Carsick Hill

A once green city, twined about the curving banks of rivers, grew
until green spaces were confined to hollows in a grid of railway lines.
Cobbles and yellow walls came interlined with brick and tarmacadam.
Green curves were city-simplified to lines laid down in concrete.
Barriers protected cars from walkers, filtered traffic into lanes.

A city, any city, cathedral quartered, virtuous at heart, may find
greed prefers virtual reality. Where hungry vessels undermine,
deep roots will break and branches wither until frail canopy remains.
A city which remembers coal, steam, furnaces, may yet forget
how fumy lungs struggle to breathe – and cut its own airline.

Stout hearts may fail, confined to grids of highway lines,
and still a wheezing city claim a sacrifice of trees.
The city covers up its ears. However many women sing
of leaves, however many green men shake their beards,
the mercenaries march its avenues and lanes.

Martin Parsons

Sheffield: Split City

I had hopes
And it was close
But my heart was rent

My beautiful city
Has closed its doors
Well, 51 percent

It scarcely seems possible
From a city so hospitable
'I came for uni, stayed for good'

A city where everyone knows
Seven Italian families
Raves to anyone who'll listen about Bragazzis

A city where neighbours pop round
With dahl and bhajis
And everybody knows Balti King do the best handees

Where underground work
Brought so many people in
And we can all pronounce Aoife, Saoirse and Fionn

But there's hurt here too
That runs deep beneath
'Europe was Thatcher's project, the nasty milk thief'

And a new wave of cold
Of post 9/11 hate
Fanatics of all types standing on Fargate

Division's just a street
Not something you should feel
Not here, not Sheffield, built upon steel

Nicky Hallett

Sound Tracks
(after Adrienne Rich)

wherever in this city   not somewhere else but here
we dream   of conversations

on Devonshire Green   on a sunny Sunday afternoon
after we've passed the kecked kebabs   from West Street's night before

the pavement smudge   of ketchup'd polystyrene trays
the undelivered papers bundled up   swollen twice as thick with rain

once we've passed the man asleep   at Rare and Racy's now-shut door
we cross Tramlines'   temporary barrier

to hunker with strangers   share the strains
of the city's   One World choir

The non-standard line spacing reflects ideas of crossing boundaries and connecting, and to mirror the effects of Adrienne Rich's work.

Veronica Fibisan

Dandelion Distribution

The unusual layout of this poem replicates the distribution of dandelions in a cross-section of the author's Sheffield garden, representing a random 1.5m by 2m cross-section surveyed via a quadrat count, the full details of which are on Veronica Fibisan's page on the *It's Our City!* website: itsoursheffield.co.uk/voices-for-change-poetry-entries.

```
                         rain ex    tin         gui
                         shes th     e g                      en's bu    zz burr
                       owed p    atterns pause                       before the city
                wa     kes forage l   egs zig-zag                     dance with
    grass spikes lig    ule                s gl            int       with pr
           om           ise       str        ata by                  height and
 coverage s      parrow      wizzes      gen    tly scoops th     golden discs as if w
   ading t           hrough      water    on the verge of    habitat   s taproots fang   lea
     ves           grow bi        tter tougher clutch the   clay wi     th childish stub   bornnes
 s b      asa    l rosett     e branches      out a stranded       chlorop   hyll seastar    fingers
                              firmly wrapped    around the         root tug bli   ndly it elongates then
   sna           ps              claws t          hat ref                         use
    to      emerge then regrow self-s          eeded they dazzle in ra   ndom distribution
          pat     terns a        cco    rding to lig   ht      and he          at frilly
 but    ton         s b      eckon    pollinators   to                    bat     he
                      in rich    cluster                        s from         creatur     e t
 o cl       um      p hous    e sparr   ow    s g    orge o    n r          ays         of
       sun     shine i             n t      he     pa                    n batte
                 r cl         ust    rs golden    sweetness              amplifi      es phyll
                    ari      es      soften prot   ein                       promis
       e i       n a        mo      uth   ful   she     ph      erd         's clock flo
   wer heads            fold lik        e broke   n u    mbrellas p    ut t
 he                                ms    elves t      o sl                              eep
    to           wa        rds eve   ning receptacle   clo            ses      pa      pp
       us            alr           ead    y b    urrowed in                the      ar
  ms of s     oothin         g w        ords ra          dio       car    rie    d o
  n the b     ree    ze       voice h              eig    hte          ne
   d and lowe   red all t    he      way do    wn bet          we                        en
                             the       jag                   ged lea           ves resonates t
                             hrough holl    ow stems a    ccu    sto            me
                      o the langu   age of    bee       s c        omb fo
              d t            oll        en wor    k meth    odi                call    y t
                   rp         ugh    ray    florets where b        ilo                 bed sti
 ro                  a matc              h the s           hape of pr     obi         ng ante
       m         ae     swi     ftly    on ano         ther w              hils       t so
              n        e             already      go                    ne          to s
 ed              cha     nge the    lan                dsc           ape    at
   pollinator   eye-lev    el seed-head plumes wor     ds        lift          the        ir d
         esc                                  ent       slo                  wed dr
           ag                        on    air for hour    s o           n e              nd
```

53

Ken Reah

Two poems for Summer

1.
Another day gone by,
And the wallflowers still not planted.

Sleek swifts deftly bank round domes of leaf-rich trees,
And, softly shrieking, slice the air with sickle wings.

2.
"Call this summer?" he says.
"You wouldn't think it was June."
"No," I said, "you wouldn't, would you?"

Our dogs, dripping,
Conduct their circular civilities, nose to tail,
Then, shaking off the surplus, go their separate ways –

So many wet things to sniff.
Through the curtain of drips round the brim of my hat
I plan my route.

The dam on my left, its surface pocked by countless small explosions.
The ducks, unfazed, glide through them – but no one's
Brought them bread, today.

The heron stands, knee-deep, waiting.
The unrelenting rain drums down upon my hat, as, exchanging rueful grins
We too separate and go our ways.

I have a Gene Kelly moment, and, with first a glance around,
dance a step or two, before the old man in me intervenes,
Before hysteria takes over.

A Dying

In a room whose window, looking down on steeples,
Made busy toys of city things,
A dying proceeded. At lunchtime.
Behind a tent of curtains, an armstretch away,
They tried to stop it. They tried
With urgent words, machines and art I did not understand.
The man with bandaged foot
Put down his head, began his lunch.
Why not? His life was saved.
But to me it seemed indelicate to eat
Within armstretch of a dying.
They worked perhaps as many minutes
As it takes to eat a modest meal. Then,
As sudden silence fell, a kestrel,
An armstretch away, flung against the sun
And flaunted a moment vivid rustglow and flickering wing
Before a graceful bank, a swoop, a swishing dive
Took it beyond.

Inside, plugs withdrawn, cylinders, tubes
Gauges removed; cutlery arranged on emptied plate.
Young men, young women, white coats
Dispersed to other cares.
No one spoke.
We seemed not to notice the curtained bed,
And tea would soon be here.

Bronwen Barber

A Clean Life

"Too clean for a buffer girl,"
was what his family said about her.
"She doesn't swear, doesn't sweat."
No silver spoon shone brighter.

They wed; soon there were five
(and a lodger) in a Pitsmoor back-to-back.
She kept it spotless, took extra turns
to wash out the courtyard privy.

He caught the slum disease. However much
she cleaned, she could not scrub away
lesions on his lungs, fever, spots of blood.
Afterwards, she took in laundry

to put food on the table. The house smarted
with Vim and Domestos. Not a speck
out of place. Dust-catching heirlooms
and treasures disappeared. "Your poems?

Your school merit certificate? In the bin.
We can do without clutter.
Cleanliness is next to Godliness."
Her granddaughter lives an ungodly life.

Abbeydale Industrial Hamlet, 31 August

A 22 of ducklings on the water
A wasp reads a poem over my shoulder

Sunlight bomb-blast flashes on the dam
Seed husks hug the millpond's edge like scum

Beech leaves jangle in the half-hearted breeze
Swallows swoop open-mouthed at flies

Silence broken by a waterwheel's creaks
Hart's-tongue licks drips in dark-filled nooks

Beating wrought-iron hooks with rhythmic clangs,
a blacksmith wakes the past with hammer and tongs

The Price of an Abbeydale Scythe

For a trade-secret formula he'd never share,
the charge of the pots and in charge of the task: Head Melter's stress

For raking out coals between running for beer,
days underground amid cool draughts and ash: Cellar Lad's cough

For treading clay barefoot for hours each day
to pound out the bubbles that'd burst as they baked: Pot Maker's leg strain

For strong arms in the sparks and an eye on the flame,
lifting up pots and skimming off muck: Puller Out's pock-marked skin

For deftly decanting the fires of Hell,
sack-apron steaming in heat that boiled blood: Teemer's bronchitis

For melding a sandwich of iron and steel,
forging crown scythes with a sharp, rhythmic thud: Hammer Man's crushed fingers

For whetting the tools as the stone flicked up dust,
giving the edge to these Sheffield-made blades: Grinder's lung disease

For black-paint protection, straw-rope wrapping last,
stainless and peerless, packed tight into crates: Finisher's sliced fingertips

For the shaking of hands on those lucrative sales
wrought from the grind of a working man's graft: Manager's death threats

For smelting a trade from the rivers and hills,
honing repute for industrial craft: Made in Sheffield

Jane Sharp

Life on the X17

The bus stops
He manoeuvres her on
Into the niche marked
Wheelchairs, prams
He puts down his bag
And sits face to face
With the woe-wizened hag
He's pushing about
'Hold on tight, ma,' he says
Won't be long, won't be long'
And begins to sing a familiar song …

The bus moves on
And he's up again
He can't sit still
His raincoat dripping
From a recent shower
His bag of shopping
Sopping wet
Incontinence pads
A bottle of pop
And wrapped round his chips
The Northern Gazette

The bus comes to a stop
And he's up again
He can't sit still
This time it's her nose
He catches the snot
In a rag from his bag
And the old woman flops
In her secondhand chair

Her curved spine in shock
Face inches from her knees
Her foot stuck at an angle on
A broken peddle
She lifts her head but it nods
Like a bobbing dog
In the back of a car
As she tries to cough

The bus sets off
And he's up again
He can't sit still
His mother's in pain
He strokes her hair
Smiles in despair
'It'll pass, ma' he says
As he tucks her in
And he turns to me
'She needs a new chair
This one's worth nothing
After *all* she's been through
Orphaned, widowed
World war two
It's not her fault
What can I do?'

The bus comes to a halt
And he's up again
He can't sit still
She's slipped an inch
Her skin feels the pinch
Her feet are skew-whiff
She's all adrift
He hoists her up
She's back in the chair
He strokes her hair

The bus is delayed
A young lad with no fare
And he's up again
He can't sit still
He fishes his wallet
Out of his bag
And pays for the lad
Then turns to me
'Go out or go mad
You know what they say
Flow with the day
I'm lucky that way
A natural optimist
That's me. Lucky
It's my middle name'

The bus changes lane
And he's up again
He can't sit still
He presses the bell
'Next stop hell,' he jokes
'Next stop hell
We're almost home, ma
A nice cup of tea.'
And he turns to me
'We're lucky to have buses
To get us about'
And he pushes her out
The bus sets off

The wonderful world
Of the X17

Off His Head

There's a crack-head in the street
I think he could be dead
He's completely stoned
Just lying there
On the new laid flags

He's a youngish guy quite tall
I think he could be dead.
People passing by
Don't really care
He's a dreg they said

In front of Marks and Spencer's
I think he could be dead
Someone shouts across
Leave him put a
Bullet in his head

There's a market stall quite near
I think he could be dead
Dial 999 help
He's off his head
And very pale, I said

The ambulance arrives
I think he could be dead
Someone knows his name
It's Dean just Dean
And no, he isn't dead

He's like this every day
The first responder said
It's spice he's on sends
Him off his head
Is that living then? I said

Paul Carnell

At Brincliffe Edge

Stock still
High on her haunches
where the steep
wooded Edge
opens to sky

Her cubs have tumbled
In these tangled hollows

Breeze flickers
licked whiskers

She's gone.

Beggar

Spare some change Guv

He's there again
Washed-up
against the subway wall.
Don't slacken.
Don't meet his eye.
There's more to this
than I dare hear.

But if (In response to *What If* by Andrew Motion on the side of the Hallam Building)

O travellers
Who pause your journey here
prepare yourselves
to climb up from Sheaf Square
and wonder at
the monolith that bears

in square cut white
a bold sans serif script
fashioned with care
intended to uplift,
to prompt our dreams
what if …?
what if …?

……… but if,

as you rise up
amidst steel and concrete
strewn as if by
some great accident,
you'll maybe think
of those that are now spent

who toiled their days
lungs clogged, throats burred,
limbs tempered
hands roughened and made hard
from beating out
the ploughshare and the sword.

From the ether
we now are ruled and fed,
we capture air
see it populated.
While we may dream
our future is connected.

Charlotte Ansell

Queen of the North

Oh my God Sheffield why
do you always leave your coat at home?
bare shouldered
and hard, you'd wear your heart on sleeves
if you had them, though you'd rather swagger
in your Santa hat
and leopard skin top, shivering on corners
with a fag. Your dreams are not in tatters

but lacquered into your big hair,
your mascara however much it's run,
you're all bluff and front,
as you sail on, invincible,
truculent and pissed,
insist your chips
are in vinegar
not on your shoulder, you snigger
at the nesh southerner on the bus wrapped

in four layers, a cardi and a scarf.
Sheffield you old tart, either shouting the odds
or a mardy bum
sulking into a shot glass, late home down ginnels
brushing away tears you carry on regardless,
even your canal
tinkles with a brittle, forced laugh,
burdened by your jewellery, the metallic glint

and wink of cars. You never let anyone into
your steely heart, you spew up your guts
from pubs and bars,
your glitter eye shadow is street lights
smudging into puddles, your neon nails
punctuating the darkness, weaving drunkenly
through a prickle of stars, your bravado
stilettos staccato on pavements.

In hope

number 73 have put deckchairs out on South Street,
surveying the Rainbow Car Wash, Akbar's, the sewage works.

Piles of fly tipping are strewn on the verge
like the rummage of a dress-up box.

The sky is soggy, a balled tissue damp with tears;
there are slug trails in the children's shoes.

I don't want them to be like me,
in needle cord flares, laughed at in the playground.

The forecast announces summer
will be back tomorrow; it may not be enough.

The accordion player on the corner in Sharrow,
is discordant with persistence not talent,

wafts of yeast and olives toss seeds of aspiration
from the windows of the Seven Hills Bakery.

In Weston Park, the ducklings have hatched,
furiously paddling to keep up.

A child's ball drops, floats to the middle of the pond.
She wills the wind to bring it back,

waits resolute against her mum's impatience
refusing to budge until it comes.

The way home is unremarked,
deckchairs flapping beneath a cold sun.

Made in Sheffield

Apprentices steered clear
of those buffer girls.
Darken their doors
and they'd have the trousers off them
rubbed down with sand and oil,
their ghosts here still,
singing, wrapped in brown paper,
mucky mouths and blacker faces,
their beauty flowered in the cutlery's shine.

He set on here at fourteen
says it's not what it were,
damp and heat might
have forced the paint
to slide off the walls
sludged with defeat,
despite the muck and grime,
the filth and fug of the forge
Rustnorstain holds true;
there's nothing leaves these doors
that doesn't gleam.

He's seen it all
cricket in the yard on dinner breaks,
how cutlery has given in
to guitars, distilled gin,
artists and God's own rugs.
Granted the dust
of the polisher's workshop
blows up all his radios,
at least one a month,
pigeons have taken over the chimney,
the rest of England could well implode
but this is Sheffield;
where phoenixes are birthed.

He wouldn't call it love,
the heft, the graft,
the hammer's pulsing thud,
furnaces ramped up, the roar,
snug, he likes to be warm.
There's no denying it's cost him,
here at six, some nights
another shift while two am
after lads came off tools at five.

He'll take the rough with the smooth,
embrace the heat, the blast,
the blaze, the ache, the push and shove,
he can tell a press is out of whack
from the other side of the yard,
knows a forge wants to be dark,
it's all in the colour,
a thousand degrees burns yella,
eight hundred and fifty's cherry red,
we all have our biting point.

Forty years forging steel,
cut to size, heat treat, shot blast,
powder coat, final grind.
There's nothing won't bend under his hands,
even the relentless cold hard weight of steel
can be coaxed, shaped and formed
with warmth, reet tools, and skill.
He'll adapt, has to or he'll brek.
May as well have letters
tattooed down his arm
like the hallmark in a knife blade:
'Made in Sheffield'.

Rita Willow

Anti – Advert (to HSBC's Poem Ad)

You stride in and strip the richness
of our city for your multiplication,
Take relish in the commodification
of the very heart of Sheffield
It's unique boldness
both its shining mettle and its
dulled mettle – strong to the core.

You don't come near to making Platinum with me –
Arctic Monkeys, Human League,
Any day, for me.
Go take your slippery songs elsewhere,
Take a brew in a bar, afar.
We are the common people
Do not kid us otherwise.

Built for Purpose

I sit here in my cool grey
stone, and worn red brick,
housing the trickle of paint,
splashes on canvas;
Firing clay, and bold bright stitchery.

Young inspired feet dash up and down
my worn stone steps, echoing my history,
my passages and stairways.

Early morning pale sun
drizzles through my thin-glazed
skylights, poking into dusty corners.

Once the hum of buffing machines
and sharp shrills from capstan lathes
pierced my chambers,
shuddered my timbers.
Oil greased the wooden floorboards,
rags hung from iron nails.

My arch opens like a generous mouth
onto this busy street corner,
welcoming artisans and visitors alike,
as I have done for centuries.
Nodding my frayed cap to little
mesters, buffer girls and labourers alike.
I am Portland Works.

On My Doorstep

Steadily I stroll through
Heeley People's Park, heading
for the Café ensconced
cosy in Heeley City Farm.
Nestled beside the Garden Centre, burgeoning
herbs – chives, rosemary, basil, thyme; and blooms –
pansies, scented geraniums, climbing clematis.

The People's Park listens to people – 'we want a
bit of the Peak District in here – millstones, rocks, heather and gorse';
'We want flower beds', 'a playground and an adventure bike track';
'climbing rocks'; 'weeping willows, seating, and mosaics'.
As I walk and appreciate the diversity
of this People's Park, I hear
the buzz of traffic on London Road, the A61,
and remember – there could have been
a bypass here! A massive dual carriageway
sweeping through our village of Heeley,
on this green hilltop.

There was going to be a bloody bypass!
Plans were all in place and approved.
Compulsory purchase made of huddled
terrace houses, people's homes; and
then demolished – en masse!

The shops and pubs along London Road
and Chesterfield Road were set to go
under the wrecking ball.

But Heeley folk spoke out –
No! We don't want this bloody
bypass – wrecking our community,
polluting our air. Traffic noise
shaking our windows. Waking our kids.
Keep The White Lion, The Red Lion;

the Motorcycle Shop, the betting shop.
The main road we've got
will do for us, to get from A to B.

Such was the volume of the campaign
that voices were heard!
Opposition to threat!
No Heeley bypass emerged.

Thankfully, I tread past heather, wildflowers,
millstones, climbing rocks, kid's playground.
Yes, a People's Park and a City Farm.
Breathe relief,
The buzz of traffic is just from the
old main road, and not from an
imposing, bloody bypass.

Molly Meleady-Hanley

It's Our City Too – Our Voice and Rights Matter Too

Multiple, youth-led movements, making a major difference across our world
> A student-led demonstration, battling climate-change now being globally unfurled

Tighter weapon-controls, increasing campaigns to stop knife-crime are also constant drives
> Two million young people marched against violence, to preserve theirs and other's lives

Democratic participation, a matter of human rights, should always to be a major political priority
> With we young people, being considered equal members of our UK democratic society.

Adults act as barriers, to stop children and young people from realising their equal rights
> Seeing children as their property, a group not to be trusted, these are ongoing slights

Speaking the right words in meetings while taking action to restrict us in their civic space
> Planning, leading and directing chosen outcomes, false inclusion, its nothing but a disgrace

Democratic participation, a fundamental right for all, is given to a selected minority
> Why aren't we, as young people, allowed to be equal members of the democratic society?

To stop our contributions, they patronise, us saying – 'All rights come with responsibilities'
> As they feign acting for our good, holding and wielding power, whilst suppressing our capabilities

These adults make wars, damage our earth and democracy, yet their rights are still preserved
> Their democratic and human rights are automatic, no matter how ill-deserved

For those of 18 plus, democratic voting, is a hard-won human right, given under UK legal authority
> Yet a change in the law, to 16, will help young people be equal members of democratic society.

No society can be considered truly democratic and participatory without meaningful inclusion
> As citizens, young people need this real proper civic platform, not some mock-up, false, illusion

Give us respectful engagement to effect change and to influence social and political places
> Let us be peers and partners in civil society, aiding improving democracy and democratic spaces

As a multicultural city, we respect and value all, let participation be our collective priority
> Young people to deserve more inclusion in the shaping of Sheffield's democratic society.

Joyce M Bullivant

Liberty stands among us all

Liberty stands among us all but yet is rarely found
In winters of oppression she lies deep within the ground
In a Northern city she stirs beneath the steely grit
fed from fire-breathing forges and deep dark claggy pit
where cold reality shows muck but seldom brass
She stirs and pushes through the air polluted grass

Our forefathers sought to make the dirt appear clean
and built workers' homes in avenues of leafy green
symbols of a kinder world and thoughts of collective good
Through Zeppelin and Blitz these freaks of Nature stood
Stunted by industrial fumes yet they stood proud
They searched for liberty and called her name out loud

Trees crash to earth but grit grinds resolve steely bright
Poll tax, ramblers' trespass, Orgreave, the massed rise to fight
In foundries of disillusion community links are forged
girding Liberty's armour from inherent memories stored
Liberty is a displaced person to those seeking power
With false news they defile her beauty hour upon hour

hidden away by those who wish she had never been
enclosed in ignorance brick by brick till then unseen
walls mortared by prejudice and selfish schemes
doors locked by false memories and bigoted dreams
Yet the little people chip till Liberty's face fast appears
And the white light of truth our unaccustomed eye sears

Liberty has no race, religion or preferred place of birth
and springs from wherever to gladly stride the earth
urging us to rejoice in the diversity that we find
Liberty is generous, thoughtful and kind.
Freedom to love our people, our country or to not
Freedom for the many to have what the few have got.

Sally Goldsmith

Fairytale

Up on the Houndkirk Road
in a foxy coat and pixie hat
with goosey snow deep enough to dream in,
a dripping sun on distant towers sparks
the edge of a corporate world
where the reds might come in the night
and jolly socialist santas bring
new mornings for all the boys and girls,
even the bad girls in their foxy coats
up on the Houndkirk Road.

Retreat to Forest Hill, 2018

The Company has privatised our Sheffield streets,
the suburbs planned and lined with limes a century ago
at careful equal spacing. Too much, the stake-outs

under trees to save them from the felling men,
and so I hide a week or so in parakeeted Forest Hill,
once taken out from commons and the Great North Wood

which stretched from Croydon to the curving Thames
and where the owners through enclosure laws forced
hermits, gypsies, charcoal men off to God knows where

though names still speak at Norwood, Honor Oak.
Now this London Borough prunes and pollards planes,
grown on streets, like Sheffield's, for the smoky city

and mends paths without axing. A text arrives from home:
the crews are out. I close my mobile phone.

The Alder, Sheffield 2017

I reach to her across their barrier:
Barbara, come on, please don't cry
I say. She loves the twin trunked alder,

its paired stems like the bond her older
sister shared with her. The tree, barred here
by the felling men, has made her cry –

such grief to lose her, the crying
then, and now, our standing here to save the alder –
it's proving more than she can bear

that they should cut it down. I stay with Barbara
and then more neighbours come. I too start to cry.
The crew look on. We gather round the alder.

Shirley Cameron

Endcliffe Park

How many parks have windows all around?
so warmly lit and oddly appearing
some at eye level and some above the ground,
three up a hill, silhouetting the trees,
several high on the cliff top,
back Psalter Lane I think;
all wrapping up the park, secure and dark but safe.
While looking out about, I see some people looking in –
through windows to the park.

Sharrow Festival in Sheffield

There is a good example in this annual Sharrow show,
Our multi-cultural city at its really very best,
With stalls for all those helpful groups,
The groups which help the world, and yet,
The gain is local, while the joy is now,
And Sarah says it's always sunny there,
Well this is true, for me I found the brightest group.
So bless the Sharrow Festival and every volunteer,
Such help for Nicaragua, and passion for the Earth, but,
It's not all great in Sheffield, though there is a lot to love,
What chance for change? We need it better run.
But still, I'd never dream of life back in the South.

The Sheaf from the Train

Such a satisfying stream,
its meanders so extreme, quite like a game,
a small boxed Amazon?
with surface taut and yellow-green,
holding down the energies,
which pour along,
        along,
                along.

It's Our City writers' workshop

This poem was written in April 2019 at the *It's Our City!* writers' workshop, run by Suzannah Evans. The poem is the result of group collaboration by Barbara Stevens, Weronika Pasieczu, Alison Teal, Mark James, Andrea Stone, Josef Palguta, Carl Douglas, Rita Willow, Abbi Flint, Sue Wright.

It's Our City!

Sit down and get o'er thi sen,
You hide the truth in your new transparent building.
Hark the herald Sheffield sings, and HSBC ran away.
We are the people who live no dreams of others,
hardworking folks with common visions.
A city grown from fields and hills,
rivers that labour for grit.
Steel streets, not gold.
See Sheffield for its shining mettle
and it's dulled mettle – strong to the core.

About *It's Our City!*

It's Our City! is a community-led network of Sheffield residents discussing and working on issues of common concern. In aiming to promote the well-being and resilience of Sheffield's diverse communities, *It's Our City!* is set up to be an independent, positive and productive contributor to local democracy.

Learn more on the *It's Our City!* website: https://www.itsoursheffield.co.uk/

If you have enjoyed this book, please consider leaving a review for the authors and editors to let them know what you thought of their work.

You can read more about this anthology on the Fantastic Books Store. While you're there, why not browse our other delightful tales and wonderfully woven prose?

www.fantasticbooksstore.com

Fantastic Books Publishing's Charity Anthologies

We have a philosophy at Fantastic Books of paying forward. We believe it is the right way to conduct daily life – personal and business. I created our first charity anthology, Fusion, with this in mind. Fusion is still going strong, still generating money for a good cause. Each one of our charity anthologies donates a percentage to a specific charity for the lifetime of the publication.

Releasing charity anthologies is a privilege and is by no means a selfless act. It has allowed us to find some of the best and brightest new writing talent while supporting a worthy cause.

Dan Grubb, CEO Fantastic Books Publishing July 2020

Fantastic Books Charity Anthologies

The Forge: Fire and Ice – a SciFan anthology that delves into the dark side and donates to Fibromyalgia Action UK

The Dummies' Guide to Serial Killing – an eclectic collection to celebrate female strength that donates to the Global Fund for Women

Synthesis – a science fiction and fantasy collection that donates to Freedom from Torture

Fusion – a science fiction and fantasy collection that donates to the World Cancer Research Fund

666 – a horror collection that donates to EDS-UK

aMUSEing Tales – a collection of children's stories that donates to the WorldWide Orphans Foundation

Ours – an international poetry collection that donates to the WorldWide Orphans Foundation

Dreaming of Steam – 23 tales of Wolds and rails that donates to the Yorkshire Wolds RailwayThe Forge: Fire and Ice, a collection of short fantasy and science fiction stories from Fantastic Books Publishing.

The Forge: Fire and Ice

is a SciFan anthology that delves into the dark side. From people on alien worlds to aliens in our world, the stories explore a multiplicity of backdrops in realms of adventure, drama, success and failure. The perils of deep space mining; a portal within a yellow bus; a mild-mannered figure bent on terrible revenge; a worm in a toffee apple; a desperate chase to find air – dystopia meets utopia, blemish meets perfection. With a Foreword by Dr Who actor, Simon Fisher-Becker.

This collection gives a charitable donation to Fibromyalgia Action UK.

The Dummies' Guide to Serial Killing
and other Fantastic Female Fables from Fantastic Books Publishing.

WINNER of the prestigious CWA Short Story Dagger 2019!

An eclectic mix of tales of female strength – from nail-biting suspense to otherworldy dilemmas; from touching portraits of personal tragedy to heart-warming stories of triumph over adversity. The Dummies' Guide to Serial Killing and other Fantastic Female Fables showcases new talent alongside seasoned professionals. It will take you on a rollercoaster of emotion from heart-stopping terror to tears of joy.

This collection gives a charitable donation to the Global Fund for Women.

Synthesis
a pure science fiction anthology
from Fantastic Books Publishing.

Foreword by Robert Llewellyn.

A collection of 27 short science fiction stories from around the globe introduced by Red Dwarf's Kryten, Robert Llewellyn.

Featuring professional contributions from
Drew Wagar, Stuart Aken and Boris Glikman.

The collection gives a charitable donation to the Freedom from Torture charity.

Fusion
**a collection of short science fiction stories
from Fantastic Books Publishing.**

A collection of twenty five stories of fantasy and science fiction from around the globe, each illustrated by digital artist Alice Taylor. This collection has been compiled from the winners of the FBP International charity short story competition 2012 and features stories from our professional contributors Danuta Reah and Stuart Aken.

*This collection gives a charitable donation to
the World Cancer Research Fund.*

666

a collection of short horror stories
from Fantastic Books Publishing.

Come one, come all and enter the realm of the 666 word story. Imagine the terrifying journey the authors went through to create a story of EXACTLY 666 words ... This is a collection of devilish, fiendish and downright pant-wetting stories from authors from around the world.

This collection gives a charitable donation to the Freedom from Torture charity.

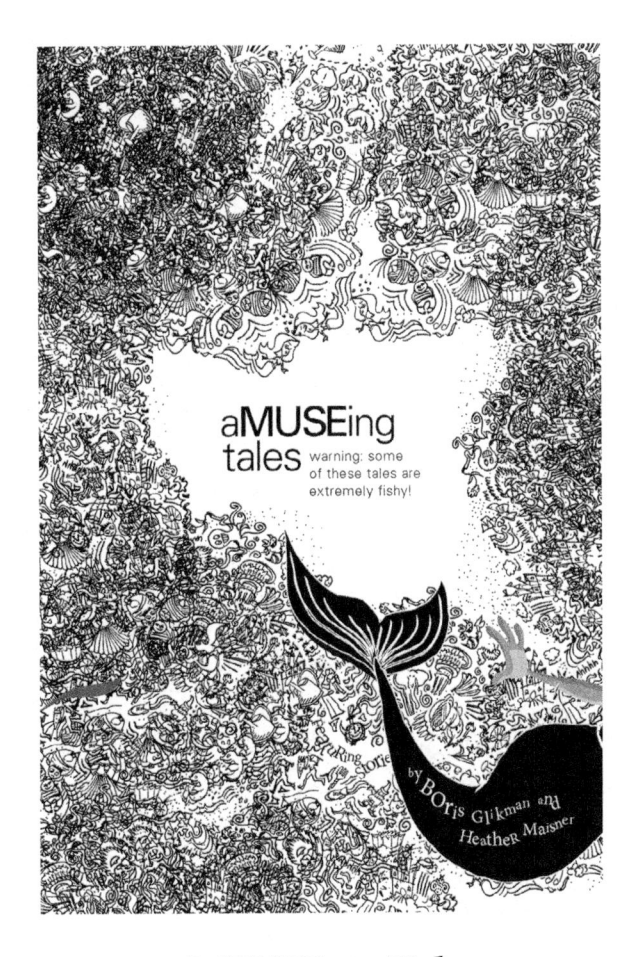

aMUSEing Tales
a collection of children's stories
from Fantastic Books Publishing.

A children's short story anthology of fourteen Fantastic stories that will fire your children's imaginations and open their eyes to worlds of dragons, mermaids, self-exploration, moral guidance and good old-fashioned fun. With fascinating cover art by Paula Murphy and professional contributions from Heather Maisner and Boris Glikman.

Enjoy these sometimes fishy but always entertaining tales!

This collection gives a charitable donation to the WorldWide Orphans Foundation.

Ours
**a collection of poetry
from Fantastic Books Publishing.**

Including a contribution from Maureen Duffy, Ours is an eclectic collection of International poetry and prose from invited poets as well as the winners of our Homeland/Motherland charity poetry competition 2013.

*This collection gives a charitable donation to
the WorldWide Orphans Foundation.*

Dreaming of Steam
a collection of short stories
from Fantastic Books Publishing.

Twenty three railway inspired tales that mine a rich seam of creativity from the heart of the Yorkshire Wolds. From pure fiction to basis in fact; from wonderfully evocative and painstaking detail to distant viewpoints, from the 1850's through to the present day and on into the future, every tale in this remarkable collection will entertain you as it brings alive the natural beauty of the Yorkshire Wolds. "The range is truly fascinating from supernatural and science-fiction to wartime drama and accounts based on real people and events" – Lord Faulkner of Worcester, President of the Heritage Railway Association

This collection gives a charitable donation to the Yorkshire Wolds Railway.

Printed in Great Britain
by Amazon